TOUCH TYPING FOR BEGINNERS

How To Type Touch, Sentence Drills, Keyboarding Practice and Lessons, Learn Touch Typing in A Quicker Time.

I0454615

ARTHUR LAMFORD

Table of Contents

PREFACE

You just arrived into the realm of touch typing! By grasping this guide, you are on the verge of embarking on a transformative journey that will transform your interaction with your computer keyboard. For students, professionals, or individuals seeking to improve their digital skills, learning and mastering touch typing can have a significant and welcoming impact. In the coming pages, the author will explain the workings of the keyboard, clarify the technique of finger positioning, and lead you through a pool of exercises specifically crafted to develop muscle memory. However, besides from the technical aspects, this book primarily focuses on empowering individuals and letting you know and cherish this beautiful skill. It pertains to attaining a proficiency that not only boosts your productivity but also exposes fresh opportunities in our technology-driven society.

ON YOUR WAY TO BECOMING COMPUTER SAVVY...

ACKNOWLEDGEMENT

I would like to use this beautiful opportunity to express my deepest gratitude to the following people, without whom this book would not have been possible; To my parents I say a beautiful thank you for your persistence support. Also, my wife, whom I love with every fiber of me, always eager to support me in any possible form. To my kids thank you for your little support. Moreover, shout out to my friends and editors, you guys are amazing.

I LOVE YOU GUYS.

CHAPTER ONE
INTRODUCTION

Let's start with the simplest question you can have about touch typing. What does it look like? It's very easy to answer this question. You can get faster if you learn how to do it. When you touch type, you type without looking at the computer. The basic idea is that each finger should rest on a different part of the keyboard. Your fingers will learn where the keys are by practicing regularly and building muscle memory, which will help you type faster in the long run. Muscle memory is vital in touch typing as it allows the fingers to find and strike the keys without conscious thought. Touch typing is very simple and can be learned quickly. You already know a simple way to touch type if you play the piano or any other instrument where you press individual keys or strings. If not, trying to play the piano is a good way to work out your fingers on both hands. You need to learn how to move each finger on its own. This can be done for five minutes at a time while watching TV. Keep going until you can press down on each finger without moving any of the others. In an electric or electronic machine, the letter printing is started by quickly and slightly depressing a key. This can also be done on a computer.

Is touch typing possible for everyone?

No. Some people aren't healthy enough to use this way of typing or even type at all on a computer. This isn't true for most people, though; it is possible for those who don't have such health problems. If you learn the right way, anyone can learn how to touch type. To keep from picking up bad habits, it's important to follow some rules as you learn to touch type. You might pick up bad habits that will hold you back if you don't.

Do most people know how to touch type?

Touch typing is a skill that almost anyone can learn, as long as they don't have any health issues. This is a skill that most people can learn. Bad habits are what can give you the wrong image. Their slow speed will make it look like you can't learn to touch type. That's the reason why you shouldn't learn them.

But how can you learn touch type without getting into bad habits? You haven't met them yet. You can't really avoid everything if you don't know how to do it. You can go slow, though. Take your time learning how to touch type.

Is touch typing no longer used?

This skill of touch typing that I'm giving you. Does it still work? Or maybe there are much better ways to type?

You already know that you don't have to type with your fingers. There are lots of other ways to type. Most of them don't work as well as touch type. There are, however, some future ways of typing that might be better than touch typing. Those ways of typing are even more complicated, and you need special training to use them correctly. However, they are tests. They don't work well with any working system and aren't stable. For example, they need a lot more work and skill than touch typing. The speeds they offer aren't something you would really need very often.

PROS OF TOUCH TYPING

Anyone who wants to learn can benefit from learning how to type by touch in many ways. The list above gives a short summary of some of them.

1. **Quickness**

Type speed is how quickly you can type on a computer. In this case, the normal working speed for a person is between 35 and 40 words per minute (WPM). A touch typist, on the other hand, can type more than 75–80 words per minute, while a hunt and peck writer would be lucky to get to 25–30 words per minute. So, touch typing can help you type quickly and get to a high speed.

2. **Accuracy**

To be accurate, you have to type the words properly, without any typos. It's an important part of touch typing just the same. With the help of touch typing, you can improve your typing speed and accuracy, which will help you get more done.

3. **Tiredness**

For sure, typing for long periods of time is a very tiring exercise. Thinking and moving around are both tired because of it. Still, touch typing makes you less tired and frees you up to focus on one thing at a time. Touch typing also saves you from having to bend your head over the computer to find the right keys.

4. **It Saves Time**

Touch typing can help you save time in your daily life by making you faster at typing, say from 30 WPM to 60 WPM. In the end, the same amount of work will be done in half the time.

5. **Your health:** People who work on a computer all day are more likely to get Repetitive Stress Injury (RSI) or Relative Strength Index (RSI). Don't worry, though; touch typing can help. When

you touch type, you don't have to bend over to use the computer, and using all of your fingers lowers your risk of RSI and other common health issues.

6. **Chances of getting a job**

Typing is no longer a skill that you can choose not to have. In fact, many companies require a certain typing speed before they will even consider hiring someone. Remember that people who can type 20 to 35 words per minute (WPM) are not recommended. One of the most useful skills you can learn for your job is how to touch type. It can help you get an entry-level job and then really do well at it so you can move up.

7. **Focus**

Finding the keys and typing are both things that need your attention when you type with two fingers. But the brain can't pay attention to two things at the same time. That's why you can focus on just one thing at a time when you touch type. At the end of the day, it increases output and lets you focus on the project's details without having to look for your keys.

8. **Editing**

You won't notice spelling or language mistakes until you make them when you type with two fingers. When you touch type, you can go back and fix any spelling or grammar problems as you go. As you type, the Backspace key makes it easy to fix mistakes.

9. Save 20 to 30 hours a month

You can type faster and save 20 to 40 hours a month if you learn how to touch type. You can now work less and spend more time with your family.

10. Stay away from RSI and inflammation

You should know that bad typing habits can lead to RSI and strains that hurt. This can be fixed by touch typing, which can also save your fingers.

11. Effectiveness

Touch typers are better at their jobs than hunt and peck typers, according to research. People who can touch type can communicate and use social media two to three times better.

12. Computer Savvy Person

A lot of work gets done faster because you can type quickly. People will think you are very good with computers and be amazed at how fast and easy you can type. A lot of the time, people are amazed by how fast I type and then ask me how they can learn to do the same.

How to type

• Keep your back straight.

• Get used to the shape of the keyboard.

• Type with your touch to begin.

• Use the right finger to press each key.

• You must always press the same finger on each key.

• Check how fast you can type to see how far you've come.

CHAPTER TWO
HOW TO BEGIN TOUCH TYPING AND WHY

Choosing the right tools and techniques to get you started.

You need to know the appropriate tools, procedures to maximize your time in learning touch typing.

Unlearn

Over the years, I became so accustomed to hunt-and-peck typing that I found it very challenging to switch to a new method. However, learning to touch type takes discipline and sacrifice; for the weeks leading up to the point where I could not type all the letters and some punctuation keys without looking at the keyboard, I typed using my dominant hand's index finger, always keeping one hand on my lap, no matter how slowly. To some, this may sound excessive, but try your hardest not to hunt and peck any more.

For starters, know the letters, period and comma

For now, don't worry about the numbers and symbols; you can quickly look them up on the keyboard. The most often used keys on the keyboard are the letters and the two punctuation keys; the sooner you become familiar with these, the better.

Food For Thought: Always pay attention to the advice given before to the start of each class. Additionally, make sure you use the finger indicator and visible keyboard to the fullest extent possible. These tools are quite helpful when you're having trouble identifying the right finger. Avoid rushing since you will become slower the faster you go. Once precision is tamed, speed will come.

Once precision is tamed, speed will come.

You should be able to type entire words and sentences in lower case without having to look at the keyboard at the end of the beginner's course. It's time to go exploring after that is finished.

Taking risks

Every day, attempt to finish at least three classes in a row without making any mistakes at all. After the learning curve becomes more manageable, extend the course, add more capital letters, and eventually enable punctuation characters. continuing with the same schedule every day.

Pro Tips

1. Keep your fingernails short.

2. For typing capital letters, hold the shift button far away from the letter you're trying to type and with the opposite hand.

3. For that one or few keys that you always keep missing, consider adding bumps to those keys, like sticking a small square piece of sellotape/Scotch tape on top of the key. So your brain knows it is reaching out for the right key.

4. Be patient.

Touch typing isn't about typing fast, it's about translating your thoughts faster, because, "If you can't move quickly enough, your idea can slip away and never come back".

Getting started with touch typing

How to type while sitting down

keep your back straight. Make sure your feet are firmly on the ground and bend both arms at a right angle.

The screen needs to be turned up so that you can face it with your head slightly tilted forward.

keep a distance of 45 to 70 cm between your eyes and the screen.

Let your wrists touch the tabletop in front of the computer to keep your shoulders, arms, and wrist muscles from getting strained. Do not rest your hands on them to shift your weight to them.

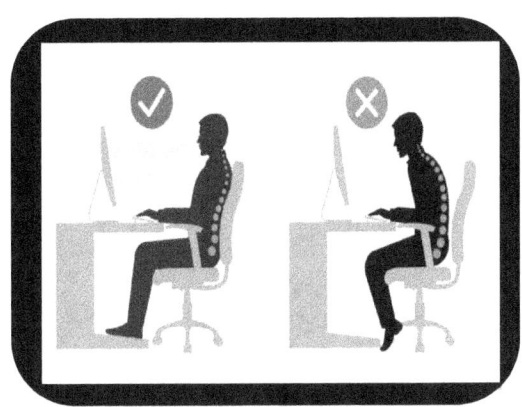

How you position yourself at your desk will determine your comfort whilst touch typing.

In particular, take heed of the following:

◆ HEAD. This should be erect. If you tilt your head forwards it puts a strain on your neck. So does watching your fingers. A poor head position can result in headaches.

◆ SHOULDERS. These should be relaxed.

◆ ELBOWS. Keep them close to your body.

◆ FINGERS. Curve your fingers, but not unnaturally so. You may need to raise your fingers more if you are using a laptop computer rather than a traditional keyboard. This is because the keys on a laptop are closer together and the keyboard itself is flatter.

◆ WRISTS. Your wrists should be flat. Aim for a straight line from the knuckles of

your middle fingers to your elbows.

◆ FEET. Keep your feet flat on the floor and do not cross your legs.

Things you should remember in general

• If at all possible, use a copyholder. Cheap ones can be bought, and they either stand on the desk or are attached to the screen. The hand chart should go on this holder at first, but eventually your work can go there too, which will keep your eyes from getting tired.

• Make sure there is enough light in the room. Where you put your equipment will depend on the rules and regulations of the office where you work. Make sure the window is behind your screen when you're at home. There shouldn't be any glare, from the sun or from lights. There is a filter that you can buy and put in front of your screen.

• Get up and down often to keep from getting stiff.

• Take breaks often—at least once every hour.

• Get your eyes checked often—every two years at the very least.

For all of the drills, use the Courier New font in 12-point size.

Each letter will take up the same amount of space, and all of your lines will end at the same place. This is called a fixed font. Double line spacing is also a good idea. This will help you see your work better. This group of eight keys is called the "Home Keys." From left to right, they are a, s, d, f, j, k, l, and; . They are in the middle of the keyboard. Your left hand's four fingers go over the a, s, d, and f. Your right hand's four fingers go over the j, k, l, and. On most keyboards, the f and j keys are marked with raised dots to make them easier to find without having to look. You should always have your fingers on these eight keys. From there, you can reach every letter, number, and symbol on the keyboard.

First, make sure that each line is perfect, and then make sure that you can type it without looking at the keys or your fingers. This is called "touch typing." It might take a while to get each line right at first, but that doesn't matter.

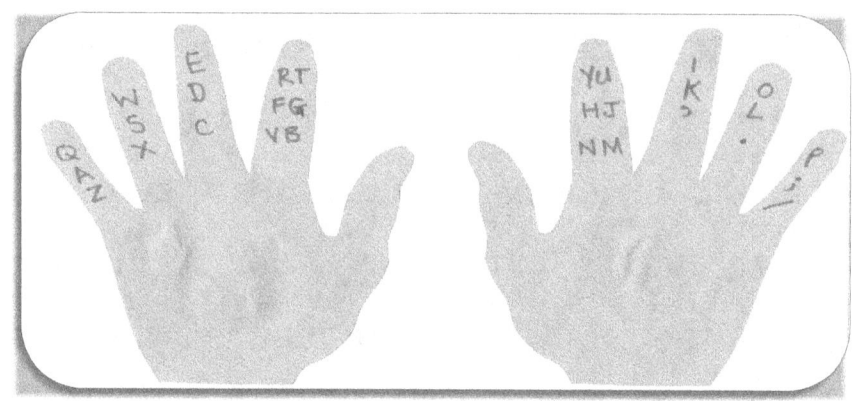

Home row position

The home row is a section of the keyboard that is central to all the other keys (see image below). Positioning your fingers over the home row allows you to more easily reach the other keys on the keyboard. When touch typing, returning your fingers to what is referred to as the '**home row position**' will assist you to type without looking at the keyboard.

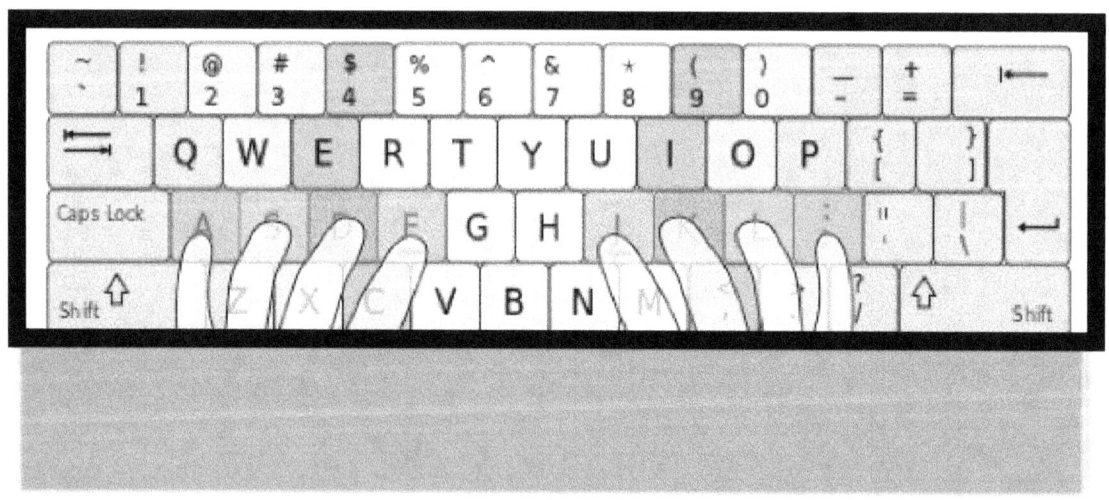

To find the spot in the home row:

1. Without looking down, find the "tabs" that are higher on the F and J keys. Put your right index finger on the J key and your left index finger on the F key.

2. Your left hand should now be on the A, S, D, and F keys, and your right hand should be on the J, K, L, and; keys.

3. Your fingers are now in the first row.

Consolidation

Remember: Type the line, check; type again if you make a mistake. No delete key to be used.

asdf jkl; asdf jkl; asdf jkl; asdf jkl; asdf jkl; asdf jkl;

fjdk sla; fjdk sla; fjdk sla; fjdk sla; fjdk sla; fjdk sla;

;lkj fdsa ;lkj fdsa ;lkj fdsa ;lkj fdsa ;lkj fdsa ;lkj fdsa

asdf jkl; asdf jkl; asdf jkl; asdf jkl; asdf jkl; asdf jkl;

all; falls fad; dad; fall sad; fads dads ask; fad all; dad;

alas ask dads fads lass lad; sad; dad; fad; falls fall all;

a jaffa asks a lad; a lad asks; all lads ask; all dads ask;

alas a dad falls; all lads; ask dad; a jaffa fad; a sad lad

all dads ask alas; a jaffa fad; dad asks a lass; ask a lad;

all lads ask; a lass asks; a jaffa asks a lass; a jaffa fad

CHAPTER THREE
LEARNING: e and i, g and h

e and i

Remember: Type the line, check, type again if you make a mistake. No delete key to be used.

◆ Use the d finger and take it up to the e

◆ Use the k finger and take it up to the i

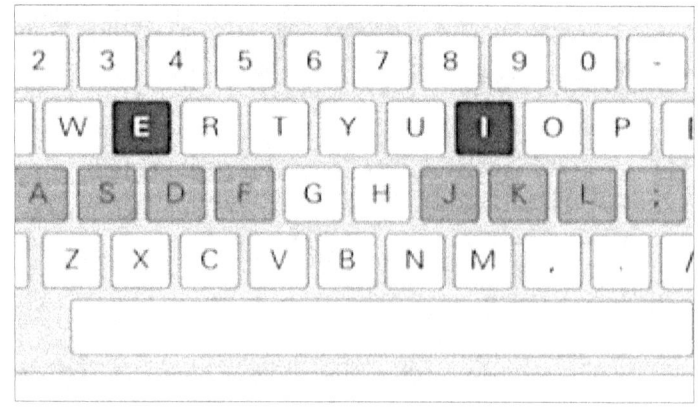

g and h

ded; ede; ded; ede; ded; ede; ded; ede; ded; ede; ded; ede;

kik; iki; kik; iki; kik; iki; kik; iki; kik; iki; kik; iki;

feed seed deed lead deal seal leak seek feel keel leek less

kill fill dill sill jill kiss kill fill dill sill jill kiss

dad kisses jill; feed a lad; feed a lass; feed all; see all

a sad seal did fall; dad filled a field; a sill leaks alas;

a lad did lie; a lass is dead; feed a seal; feed a deaf lad;

feed a seal leeks; seek a lead; feed jill a leak; feel sad;

ask a deed; a sill leaks; jill falls ill; jaffa kisses jill

fill a seed field; ask less if jill is sad; all lasses fall

Remember: Type the line, check; type again if you make a mistake. No delete key to be used.

- Use the f finger and take it across to the g

- Use the j finger and take it across to the h

Consolidation

Remember: Type the line, check, type again if you make a mistake. No delete key to be used.

fill a seed field; ask less if jill is sad; all lasses fall

ask a deed; a sill leaks; jill falls ill; jaffa kisses jill

feed a seal leeks; seek a lead; feed jill a leek; feel sad;

a lad did lie; a lass is dead; feed a seal; feed a deaf lad

a sad seal did fall; dad filled a field; a sill leaks alas;

dad kisses jill; feed a lad; feed a lass; feed all; see all

i sigh like jill; jed has a high hall; see jaffa as he jigs

jill digs a field; jill likes a hike; a gas leak kills all;

i like a fig; half a heel has held; jill has a gash; i hike

he held a jaffa as he fell; add a high gas; dig a fig field

a lass sighed; see a high hill; has he held a seal; i asked

he liked a jig; she liked a jig; all liked a jig; see a jig

LEARN: o and n, shift keys and t

o and n

Remember to type the line, check it, and type it again if you messed up. You can't use the delete key.

-Take your l finger and bring it up to your o finger.

- Put your j finger on the n and pull it down.

lol; olo; lol; olo; lol; olo; lol; olo; lol; olo; lol; olo;

jnj; njn; jnj; njn; jnj; njn; jnj; njn; jnj; njn; jnj; njn;

dog; hog; fog; log; nog; jog; goon soon loon noon lose hose

nose dose none gone lone line fine dine sign nine lane sane

a lad had a fine dog; he held his lead; he jogged in a lane

fog had soon hidden all signs of a field; he fell on a log;

she had a fine salad and half of a fish; she soon had none;

he had a fine nose; she had gone insane; she had a fine fig

sad lad and his dog had gone jogging in a field and he fell

jed dosed on a log; he soon had no dog; he had gone inside;

Shift keys and t

Remember to type the line, then check it. If you make a mistake, type it again. You can't use the delete key.

- Press the shift keys with your little finger. To type a single capital letter, press the shift key. The caps lock key is better if you need to type a lot of capital letters, like in a heading.

- To type a capital letter on the left side of the keyboard, use your right little finger, and to type a capital letter on the right side, use your left little finger.

Ask; See; Don; Fog; Gas; Had; Jag; Keg; Leg; Nag; All; Sag;

tag; tog; tin; ton; tan; ten; tea; tie; toll tall till tell

That Kill Fill Sell Till Hill Gill Doll Noel Tent Hide Tide

Lilt Hilt Silt Tilt Kilt Gilt Talk Gate Hate Fate Late Date

I said I hated the doll and that I felt it had a tin leg;

She talked of Noel and said she asked if he hated jogging

Ask to see Don and see if he sells gates; tents and dolls

I said I felt fine and that I jogged in a field at night;

He let his dog loose in the field and he fished in a lake

The fog had filled the field and I fell on a sagging log;

- Bring your j finger up to your t.

Consolidation

Remember: Type the line, check; type again if you make a mistake. No delete key to be used.

```
jed dosed on a log; he soon had no dog; he had gone inside;

the lad and his dog had gone jogging in a field and he fell

he had a fine nose; she had gone insane; she had a fine fig

she had a fine salad and half of a fish; she soon had none;

fog had soon hidden all signs of a field; he fell on a log;

a lad had a fine dog; he held his lead; he jogged in a lane

The fog had filled the field and I fell on a sagging log;

He let his dog loose in the field and he fished in a lake

I said I felt fine and that I jogged in a field at night;

Ask to see Don and see if he sells gates; tents and dolls

She talked of Noel and said she asked if he hated jogging

I said I hated the doll and that I felt it had a tin leg;
```

LEARN: extra practice. and y

Extra practice

Remember: Type the line, check; type again if you make a mistake. No delete key to be used.

. and y

Remember: Type the line, check, type again if you make a mistake. No delete key to be used.

◆ Use the l finger and take it down to the '.'

◆ Use the j finger and take it up to the y.

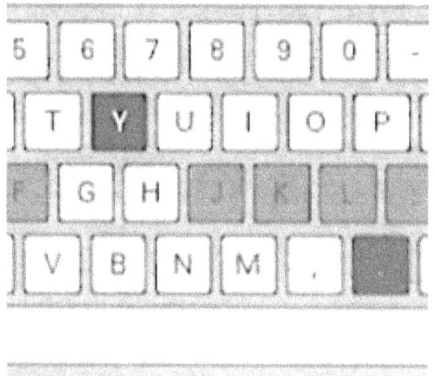

hyn; yhn; nhy; hyn; yhn; nhy; hyn; yhn; nhy; hyn; yhn; nhy;

lo. ol. .lo lo. ol. .lo lo. ol. .lo lo. ol. .lo lo. ol. .lo

Yet. Yes. Yen. Nay. Hay. Gay. Say. Lay. Kay. Joy. Toy. Eye.

yell they flay slay yank yoke yolk toys eyes says nays lays

They all liked seeing the toys shining gaily on a shelf.

The lads yelled as they yanked the leg of a little lass.

I said that they yelled in joy at the toys on the shelf.

His eyes said it all. He talked of this feeling of hate.

The yolks of the little eggs lay shining in the toy tin.

Slay the nasty hog. Lay it on the shelf in the tool shed

Consolidation

Remember: Type the line, check, type again if you make a mistake. No delete key to be used.

She felt the fog lift late as she jogged into the field;

He talked of the fate of those dolls; I said I felt fine

She had no sign of the noon fog; The lane had soon gone;

Half of a fish had hidden in the sea; she held his head;

Dad gashed his leg; a lad held a fig; see a jaffa field;

He likes a dig; she likes a dig; all liked a dig; a lass

Slay the nasty hog. Lay it on the shelf in the tool shed

The yolks of the little eggs lay shining in the toy tin.

His eyes said it all. He talked of this feeling of hate.

I said that they yelled in joy at the toys on the shelf.

The lads yelled as they yanked the leg of a little lass.

They all liked seeing the toys shining gaily on a shelf.

LEARN: , and w rand b

, and w

Remember: Type the line, check; type again if you make a mistake. No delete key to be used.

- Use the k finger and take it down to the ,
- Use the s finger and take it up to the w

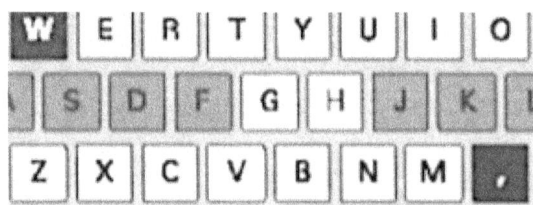

ik, ,ki ki, ik, ,ki ki, ik, ,ki ki, ik, ,ki ki, ik, ,ki ki,

wsw sws wsw sws wsw sws wsw sws wsw sws wsw sws wsw sws wsw

way, was, wag, wan, wad, wet, wed, won, wok, wow, win, wig,

wall well will west wash wish wind wand when wean week weak

Ask the lady who was at the Dog Show to talk to the lad.

We talked, we walked, we went in to tea, then we waited.

We will wait while the lady talks to the tall, weak lad.

What was the lad doing, whistling at those wagging dogs.

We won the shiny toy, yet we did not win the tin shield.

Wash the wig, so that she will want to look at it again.

r and b

Remember: Type the line, check, type again if you make a mistake. No delete key to be used.

◆ Use the f finger and take it up to the r

◆ Use the f finger and take it down to the b

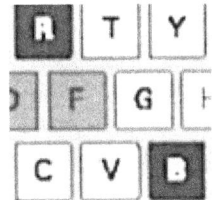

⟵──────────────────────────────────────⟶

frf rfr frf rfr frf rfr frf rfr frf rfr frf rfr frf rfr frf

bgb gbg bgb gbg bgb gbg bgb gbg bgb gbg bgb gbg bgb gbg bgb

beat bear bead beak bean been beef bell bill bass bees boil

reel reef read reek roll rash rest root roof ride raid reed

There were lots of boys in the band and they enjoyed it.

The bread and rolls in the store had been there all day.

The bread baked in the kiln tasted better than the rest.

We had been riding the bikes all week and we were tired.

The bear reeked of beef stew so we beat a hasty retreat.

Billy had been rolling on the floor; he was boiling hot.

Consolidation

Remember: Type the line, check, type again if you make a mistake. No delete key to be used.

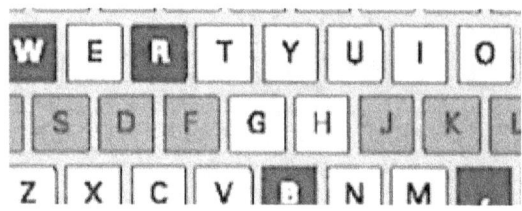

Wash the wig, so that she will want to look at it again.

We won the shiny toy, yet we did not win the tin shield.

What was the lad doing, whistling at those wagging dogs.

We will wait while the lady talks to the tall, weak lad.

We talked, we walked, we went in to tea, then we waited.

Ask the lady who was at the Dog Show to talk to the lad.

Billy had been rolling on the floor; he was boiling hot.

The bear reeked of beef stew so we beat a hasty retreat.

We had been riding the bikes all week and we were tired.

The bread baked in the kiln tasted better than the rest.

The bread and rolls in the store had been there all day.

There were lots of boys in the band and they enjoyed it.

LEARN: m and u p and c

m and u

Remember: Type the line, check, type again if you make a mistake. No delete key to be used.

◆ Use the j finger and take it down to the m

◆ Use the j finger and take it up to the u

jmj mjm jmj mjm jmj mjm jmj mjm jmj mjm jmj mjm jmj mjm jmj

juj uju juj uju juj uju juj uju juj uju juj uju juj uju juj

mast mash mars mats mail meal mile mole moon mend mind mint

burn turn lure fuss dust rust must gust lust gush lush mush

My older brother kindly mended my new motor bike for me.

I must shut the toilet door and remember to use the key.

We must make our dinner more interesting and nourishing.

The wind gusted, and the mast blew around the main roof.

My mum mended the sagging hems. It was most kind of her.

The main meal of the day was roast beef and baked beans.

p and c

Remember: Type the line, check; type again if you make a mistake. No delete key to be used.

- Use the; finger and take it up to the p
- Use the d finger and take it down to the c

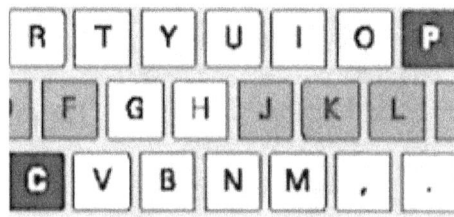

;p; p;p ;p; p;p ;p; p;p ;p; p;p ;p; p;p ;p; p;p ;p; p;p ;p;

edc cdc edc cdc edc cdc edc cdc edc cdc edc cdc edc cdc edc

pool push pump purl pram prim pram palm peel pure paid pile

cart curt corn core cure care coal cash cell call clot clad

The policeman pushed his cycle by the tall church clock.

Appropriate care must be taken when photocopying papers.

The prim and proper nanny pushed the pram down the path.

Take care of the cash. Call David and pay him a portion.

Pull the pump up carefully and the water will spurt out.

The cart crashed past as it caught the edge of the path.

Consolidation

Remember: Type the line, check, type again if you make a mistake. No delete key to be

Used.

The main meal of the day was boiled beef and mushy peas.

My mum mended the sagging hems. It was most kind of her.

The wind gusted, and the mast blew around the main roof.

We must make our dinner more interesting and nourishing.

I must shut the toilet door and remember to use the key.

My older brother kindly mended my new motor bike for me.

The cart crashed past as it caught the edge of the path.

Pull the pump up carefully and the water will spurt out.

Take care of the cash. Call David and pay him a portion.

The prim and proper nanny pushed the pram down the path.

Appropriate care must be taken when photocopying papers.

The policeman pushed his cycle by the tall church clock.

LEARN: v and x q and z

v and x

Remember: Type the line, check, type again if you make a mistake. No delete key to be used.

◆ Use the f finger and take it down to the v
◆ Use the s finger and take it down to the x

rfv vfv rfv vfv rfv vfv rfv vfv rfv vfv rfv vfv rfv vfv rfv

wsx xsw wsx xsw wsx xsw wsx xsw wsx xsw wsx xsw wsx xsw wsx

vent vein vane vine view vole vale veil vile vice vest vamp

oxen exit axis hoax taxi coax box, fox, cox, pox, fax, tax,

A vexed taxi man viewed the jam with extreme impatience.

The extra climb gave a better view over the next valley.

The exit was hidden from the view of the old van driver.

The fox jumped over the exit box and captured the voles.

It was a police hoax and the vice teams were very vexed.

Victoria views paying road taxes with very vivid hatred.

q and z

Remember: Type the line, check; type again if you make a mistake. No delete key to be used.

- Use the a finger and take it up to the q

- Use the a finger r and take it down to the z

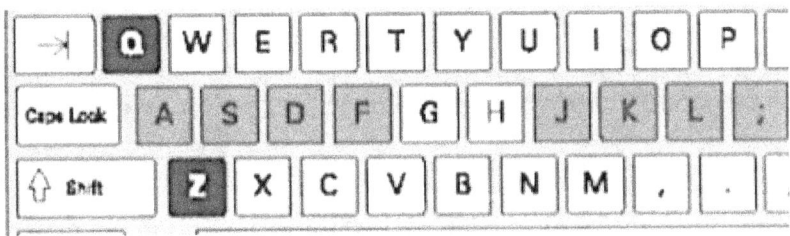

qaz aqa qaz aqa qaz aqa qaz aqa qaz aqa qaz aqa qaz aqa qaz

zaq aza zaq aza zaq aza zaq aza zaq aza zaq aza zaq aza zaq

aqua quit quay quid quod quiz quip quaint quota equal quell

zoom zeal zest haze maze gaze laze fuzz buzz zulu lazy hazy

Jo at the zoo asked quite odd questions about the zebra.

The lady gazed at the buzzing bee down by the boat quay.

He quit the jobs because he was a lazy and quiet worker.

In order to coax Xavier to eat he devised a quaint plan.

In the lazy, hazy days of summer it is quite often warm.

The buzzy bee zoomed around the lazy queen as she cried.

Consolidation

Remember: Type the line, check, type again if you make a mistake. No delete key to be used.

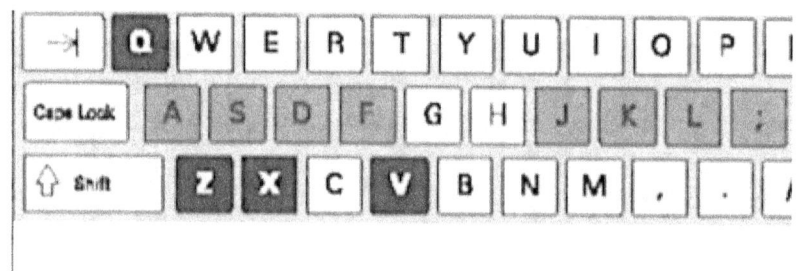

Victoria views paying road taxes with very vivid hatred.

It was a police hoax and the vice teams were very vexed.

The fox jumped over the exit box and captured the voles.

The exit was hidden from the view of the old van driver.

The extra climb gave a better view over the next valley.

A vexed taxi man viewed the jam with extreme impatience.

The buzzy bee zoomed around the lazy queen as she cried.

In the lazy, hazy days of summer it is quite often warm.

In order to coax Xavier to eat he devised a quaint plan.

He quit the jobs because he was a lazy and quiet worker.

The lady gazed at the buzzing bee down by the boat quay.

Jo at the zoo asked quite odd questions about the zebra.

CHAPTER FOUR
LEARN: SENTENCE DRILLS

When it comes to touch typing, being able to make smooth, accurate keystrokes is key to being more productive and efficient. Sentence drills are a powerful tool that can help you get to this level of proficiency. Structured exercises called sentence drills are meant to improve typing skills by focusing on using learned keys in real-life sentences. We'll talk about the benefits of sentence drills and how adding them to your typing practice can help you get much better.

Why sentence drills are important

1. Learning in Real Life: Sentence drills are a useful and real-life way to learn how to type. Instead of doing the same letters or words over and over, sentence drills put the typist in real-life situations and help them connect the dots between individual keystrokes and the formation of full sentences.

2. Better accuracy: Typing full sentences helps students get a better sense of rhythm and flow, which leads to better accuracy. Continuously combining different keys in a sentence helps build muscle memory, cut down on mistakes, and improve overall accuracy.

3. Speed Improvement: Doing sentence drills is a great way to improve your typing speed. Typist naturally get faster without losing accuracy as they move through drills. Typists are forced to think ahead as sentences get more complicated over time, which makes them type faster and more efficiently.

What you need to know to use sentence drills in your practice

1. Start Easy: People who are just starting out should start with simple sentences that use the new keys they've learned. This lets the level of difficulty build slowly, making sure that you have a strong base before moving on to more difficult drills.

2. Pay attention to common phrases: Use everyday words and phrases that are relevant to your typing needs. This not only improves your typing skills, but it also gets you ready for typing tasks you'll face in real life, like writing emails or documents.

3. Keep track of your progress: Write down how well you did on sentence drills. Keep an eye on your words per minute (WPM) and accuracy on a regular basis to see how you're doing and figure out what areas might need more work.

4. Use software to type: Use software for typing that has structured sentence drills. There are many typing programs that have lessons that are designed to make learning to type sentences

fun and easy. This will make it easier for you to use this technique every day.

5. Do Other Exercises Along with Sentence Drills: Sentence drills are helpful on their own, but they can be even more helpful when done with other typing exercises. To make a well-rounded training plan, do both traditional exercises and drills as part of your daily practice.

Sentence Drills

Remember: Type the line, check, type again if you make a mistake. No delete key to be used.

I came up with these set of sentence drills for touch typing, covering each letter from A to Z:

A - "Anderson's agile cat always acrobatically avoids any alarming ants."

B - "Bright blue birds build beautiful nests behind the bustling bakery."

C - "Curious children carefully collect colorful shells on the calm coast."

D - "Dancing daffodils delightfully decorate the dew-kissed dawn."

E - "Every evening, energetic elephants elegantly explore the emerald expanse."

F - "Fragrant flowers fill the forest, fascinating foxes and friendly fawns."

G - "Graceful gazelles gracefully glide across the golden grasslands."

H - "Happy hummingbirds hum harmoniously, hovering over hibiscus blooms."

I - "In icy inlets, intrepid iguanas investigate intriguing icebergs."

J - "Jubilant jugglers joyfully juggle jewel-toned juggling balls."

K - "Kindergarten kids keenly kick kites in the kite-flying contest."

L - "Lively ladybugs lazily lounge on large, leafy lemon leaves."

M - "Mysterious moonlit meadows mesmerize magical midnight moose."

N - "Nimble ninja newts navigate narrow, noisy, nocturnal neighborhoods."

O - "Overhead, orange orioles orchestrate an opulent, optimistic opera."

P - "Playful penguins perform perfectly synchronized pirouettes."

Q - "Quaint quokkas quietly quibble near the quaint, quiet quay."

R - "Radiant rainbows regularly reveal remarkable, rare rainforest reptiles."

S - "Silly squirrels skillfully snatch shiny, scrumptious acorns."

T - "Tiny turtles tactfully tiptoe through tall, tangled tulips."

U - "Underneath the umbrella, ukulele-playing unicorns utter unique tunes."

V - "Vibrant violets vividly bloom in valleys, valleys very vast."

W - "Whistling winds whisper within willow trees, waltzing with white-winged warblers."

X - "Xylophones xerox xenophobic x-ray technicians in a perplexing mix."

Y - "Yellow yaks yodel yuletide yodels while yawning in the yurt yard."

Z - "Zany zebras zealously zigzag through the zesty, zigzagging zoo."

I designed these sentences to include each letter of the alphabet, providing an amusing and varied set of drills for touch typing practice.

KEYBOARDING PRACTICE: SENTENCE REPETITION

By practicing these sentences, you will get a good feel for the most common keys and continue to learn how to use the keyboard. Make sure you don't look at the keyboard while you type. When you don't have to look at your hands, you can focus on the screen and do things faster and more accurately. This is what you need to do: type each sentence 15 times; then type those sentences again 10 more times, making sure you get all the words right. As an extra challenge, try typing all of your sentences faster after you're done with the ones that don't have any mistakes. Work on any words that are wrong, and then type those sentences 10 times more.

SENTENCES:

1. Please go for a short walk with your dog Cali; he needs it badly!

2. What a beautiful day to be on the beach in Hawaii, where it's nice and bright.

3. The renowned scientist Rex Quinfrey made plans for a machine that would make people invisible.

4. Do you know why all of those chemicals are so bad for the environment?

5. Why didn't you tell me how many copper pennies were in that jar?

6. Max Justin drove his car around every corner in a sneaky way to find his dog.

7. The two boys gathered sticks outside in the bitter cold for more than an hour!

8. When do you think they'll be back from their trip to Cairo, Egypt?

9. Our cats, Trixie and Veronica, love to play with their pink yarn ball.

10. It took us just under two hours to get to the top of the mountain. Isn't that great?

11. Hiliary questioned Mr. Victor for two hours but couldn't find out anything.

12. Today I need to wash my car, call my mom, and feed my dog.

12. Xavi Paul saw sixty big boxes and sixteen little boxes stacked outside.

14. On Thursday, the Richard family chose to visit an amusement park.

15. It looks like that group of bison is moving quickly. Is that normal?

16. All of the grandfather clocks in that store were set to 4 o'clock.

17. France has a lot of great vacation spots, like Paris, Rome, Prague, and more.

18. That jewellery with those diamonds and rubies will look lovely.

19. It looked like the steamboats were moving very slowly down the Mississippi River.

20. Ziko would have to work all night to keep up with that speed.

SPEED BOOSTERS

Making yourself type simple sentences over and over will help you get faster. That will help you type quickly without stopping. Don't believe me? Type speed tests can help you decide. You can go over this part more than once and then keep track of your progress. The steps are as follows: type each sentence ten times; then type those sentences ten more times, making sure you get all the words right each time.

SPEED BOOSTING SENTENCES

1. A bird in the hand is worth two in the bush.

2. Being stuck between two things that are not good.

3. Locking the barn door again after the horse gets out.

4. Do I look like a turnip that got off the truck?

5. Don't give up hope before the eggs are laid.

Sixth, don't make a big deal out of nothing.

7. Friends are like flowers in a garden.

8. On the other side, the grass is always greener.

9. Staying one day ahead of yesterday.

10. Sleep with dogs and get fleas when you wake up.

11. The wine is sweeter when the berry is sour.

12. The person who makes the most noise gets the oil.

13. The trees get stronger when the wind blows hard.

14. You can get to a man's heart through his stomach.

15. A weed is really just a flower that wears a different color.

16. That's something we'll deal with when it comes up.

17. You can show a horse water, but not make it drink.

18. Old dogs can't learn new things.

19. Life isn't fun if you don't have any fun.

20. Your car is old as soon as you pay for it.

MORE

The swift brown fox skips over the sluggish dog.

Pack my box with five dozen liquor jugs.

Jinxed wizards pluck ivy from the big quilt

How razorback-jumping frogs can level six piqued gymnasts!

Crazy Fred bought many very exquisite opal jewels

Mrs Joyce, TV quiz PhD, bags few lynx.

Paulina love my big sphinx of quartz.

phinx of black quartz, judge my vow.

The five boxing wizards jump quickly.

Bright vixens jump; dozy fowl quack.

CHAPTER FIVE

FIGURES

Figures

Remember: Type the line, check, type again if you make a mistake. No delete key to be used.

```
de3ed  de3d  d3d  de3ed  de3d  d3d  de3ed  de3d  d3d  de3ed  de3d

ju7uj  ju7j  j7j  ju7uj  ju7j  j7j  ju7uj  ju7j  j7j  ju7uj  ju7j

fr4rf  fr4f  f4f  fr4rf  fr4f  f4f  fr4rf  fr4f  f4f  fr4rf  fr4f

ki8ik  ki8k  k8k  ki8ik  ki8k  k8k  ki8ik  ki8k  k8k  ki8ik  ki8k

aqlqa  aqla  ala  aqlqa  aqla  ala  aqlqa  aqla  ala  aqlqa  aqla

sw2ws  sw2s  s2s  sw2ws  sw2s  s2s  sw2ws  sw2s  s2s  sw2ws  sw2s

jy6yj  jy6j  j6j  jy6yj  jy6j  j6j  jy6yj  jy6j  j6j  jy6yj  jy6j

fr5rf  fr5f  f5f  fr5rf  fr5f  f5f  fr5rf  fr5f  f5f  fr5rf  fr5f

lo9ol  lo9l  l9l  lo9ol  lo9l  l9l  lo9ol  lo9l  l9l  lo9ol  lo9l

;p0p;  ;p0;  ;0;  ;p0p;  ;p0;  ;0;  ;p0p;  ;p0;  ;0;  ;p0p;  ;p0;

1qaz  2wsx  3edc  4rfv  5tgb  6yhn  7ujm  8ik,  9ol.  0p;/  1qaz.

zaq1  xsw2  cde3  vfr4  bgt5  nhy6  mju7  ,ki8  .lo9  /;p0  zaq1.
```

3 duds 33 dots 3 dons 33 dogs 3 duds 33 dots 3 dons 33 dogs

7 jugs 77 jars 7 jams 77 jigs 7 jugs 77 jars 7 jams 77 jigs

4 figs 44 feet 4 fees 44 fans 4 figs 44 feet 4 fees 44 fans

8 kits 88 keys 8 kids 88 kegs 8 kits 88 keys 8 kids 88 kegs

This job lot was: 11 woollen suits, 1 blouse and 11 collars

2 saws 22 sons 2 suns 22 sets 2 saws 22 sons 2 suns 22 sets

6 jays 66 jobs 6 jets 66 jabs 6 jays 66 jobs 6 jets 66 jabs

5 fins 55 fibs 5 fags 55 firs 5 fins 55 fibs 5 fags 55 firs

9 logs 99 lads 9 lots 99 laws 9 logs 99 lads 9 lots 99 laws

20 pages; 30 pills; 40 papers 20 pages; 30 pills; 40 papers

The man caught 26 pike, 15 roach, 36 tiddlers and 2 plaice.

Jane got 16 marks in geography and just 14 marks in French.

Consolidation

Remember: Type the line, check, type again if you make a mistake.
No delete key to be used

```
There were 3 dogs, 33 cats, and 330 hamsters at the park.

I saw 7 people on Monday, 77 on Tuesday, and 7 yesterday.

Weigh out 4 oz of flour, 4 oz of sugar, and add the eggs.

At 8 o'clock I went out to see the 88 horses at the show.

I had 1 suit, 1 pair of trousers, 1 skirt and 11 jumpers.

The 2 of us saw 2 plays at the theatre on the 22nd August.

If you add 6 and 6 and 6 you will find the right answers.

1 think 5 is a nice round figure; 5 people and 5 animals.

On the 9th September we went out at 9 pm in 9 cranky cars.

The value is 0, but we really need a value of 100 or 200.

Jane had 239 bars of chocolate, 56 lollies and 76 sweets.

Add 569 to the totals of 890 and then you will have 1459.
```

CHAPTER SIX

ALPHABETICAL PARAGRAPHS

Remember: Type the paragraph, check, type again if you make a mistake. No delete key to be used.

When you touch type, accuracy is very important. It can be hard for beginners to find the right keys. Backspace is a key that lets you quickly fix mistakes. For touch typing to work well, your hands need to be in a comfortable position. A big part of getting good at touch typing is building muscle memory. Ergonomics is a big part of keeping people from getting stressed. For fastest typing, keep your fingers on the home row keys. As you feel more confident, slowly speed up your typing. The home row keys are the building blocks of touch typing. Consistent practice will help you get better at being accurate. Typing speed goes up as you get better at it and use the keyboard more. The layout of keyboards is standard so that touch typing works well. Use keyboard shortcuts to speed up the process of typing. It takes time and effort to get good at touch typing. A separate set of keys called a numeric keypad lets you enter numbers. The best place to put your hand when touch typing cuts down on mistakes. Regularly practicing touch typing will help you get faster and more accurate. Paying attention to the right way to type will improve the quality of your work.

As you get better at touch typing, rhythm and flow start to form. Having muscle memory makes you fast naturally. When you first start touch typing, technique is more important than speed. Don't get tired by putting your fingers in the wrong places. Typing faster comes with a lot of practice. When you're typing for long periods of time, wrist rests can help relieve stress. The X and Z keys are built into the keyboard. If you put in the work, you'll get better at touch typing. Focus on certain areas to get better at them. In this digital world, being able to touch type is a useful skill.

More Work with Sentences

Remember to type the line, check it, and type it again if you messed up. You can't use the delete key.

1. The quick brown fox jumps over the slow dog.

2. Jaguars love my big quartz sphinx.

3. Gymnasts are interested in how razorback-jumping frogs can get to level six!

4. Put fifty liquor jugs in my box.

5. Mr. Jock, a TV quiz show host with a PhD, gets a few lynx.

6. Cwm fjord bank glyphs vext test.

7. Sphinx of black quartz, look at my promise.

8. There are five boxing wizards who jump very high.

9. Glib jocks test nymph to annoy dwarf.

10. The vampire fox only held the quartz duck by its wings.

11. Wizards who are cursed take ivy from the big quilt.

12. Little things are what make life worth living.

13. It only takes one step to start a journey that lasts a thousand miles.

14. Success isn't final, and failure isn't the end. What matters is having the courage to keep going.

15. Our doubts today will be the only thing stopping us from realizing what we want to do tomorrow.

16. If you think you can do it, you'll get there.

17. You don't have to plan for life to happen. It does.

18. Don't strike the iron when it's already hot; strike it to make it hot.

19. You can only do great work if you love it.

20. Chances can be found in the middle of trouble.

Remember to focus on accuracy at first, and then slowly speed up as you get used to where the keys are. Over time, practicing these sentences regularly will help you get better at touch typing.

SENTECNCE PRATICE WITH NUMBERS

1. Jump over the lazy dog! 1, 2, 3, Go!

2. The quick brown fox jumps 5 feet high.

3. We needed 6 cars, 8 motor bikes and 10 scooters to race.

4. George scored 689, Alan scored 786 and Peter scored 876

5. 7 days a week, 24 hours a day.

6. Ask for 1 tie, 2 shirts, 3 jackets and 4 jumpers

7. 9 out of 10 users recommend this product.

8. I spent 6 hours a day, practicing coding.

9. The password must be at least 8 characters long.

10. She scored 97% on her typing test.

11. The meeting is scheduled for 2:30 p.m. sharp!

These sentences provide a mix of letters, numbers, and special characters to help users practice touch typing across the keyboard.

PARAGRAPH PRACTICE

Remember to type the paragraph, look it over, and type it again if you messed up. You can't use the delete key.

START

Christian Johny did a great job driving the car. From 0 to 65 mph in no time, he was a very fast driver. But he seemed to know what he was doing, and I always felt safe with him.

The bee flew around the purple flowers. It was a pretty bright color and made a lot of noise. I was about to start using my rake nearby when I heard a buzzing sound. I had to stop because I are afraid of bees.

Josephine had signed up for the relay race. The young woman was pretty and eager, but she ran very slowly, and the other people on the team didn't like how she tried to help them.

ANOTHER EXAMPLE

It was both an amazing and terrible day. Things were pretty calm at first, but then everything went crazy. It wasn't until evening that things were back to normal. We had already been through enough excitement for one day by that point.

Zack behaved perfectly throughout the whole thing. She knew exactly when to get the information from him, but he passed out right before she did it. It was too late when she quickly reached him.

Lots of people were having fun all over the park. It was a nice, warm day for lounging around. The swings, climbing frame, and slides got the kids very excited. Everything looked good and everyone was happy.

See More Examples

1. Getting Started: Practice in the home row First, put your fingers gently on the keys in the middle row. For the left hand, use ASDF and for the right hand, use JKL. Use the keys on the first row to type the words "sad dad salad lads flask glass had had." Try to keep a steady pace as you move your fingers over the keys. Feel the rhythm.

2. Alphabet Adventure: A Trip Around the QWERTY World Use your fingers to go on a trip through the alphabet. Pay close attention to where each letter is on the keyboard as you type the following sentences: "Quickly jump over lazy dogs." A fox is quick and dark brown. The strange bird took off. Take pleasure in the challenge of getting to know the QWERTY landscape.

3. Word Harmony: How to Get Your Typing to Flow Type these phrases together without any breaks: "The quick brown fox jumps over the lazy dog." Jill and Jack went up the hill. If a woodchuck could chuck wood, how much would it throw?" Let the words come out naturally as you get your thoughts and typing to work together.

4. Figurative Language: Dancing with Unique Characters Jump into the world of signs! "Let's meet at 3:30 pm, and don't forget to bring your $10 for the movie ticket!" Type the following sentence using letters and symbols. Learn how to use the Shift key and other modifier keys to make your typing sound more rhythmic.

Race Against Time in Speed Boost Timed exercises are a great way to push yourself. Time yourself for three minutes and type this sentence as quickly and correctly as you can: "As the sun goes down behind the mountains, it casts a warm glow across the valley." After the birds go back to their nests, it's a quiet evening everywhere. Don't stress about making mistakes; just work on getting faster.

6. Troubleshooting Journey: How to Correct Mistakes with Style Accept that mistakes are going to happen. "This quick-brown fox jumps over that lazy dog." Type the following sentences while making sure they are correct. It was a lovely day in the neighborhood. Now, go back and fix each mistake. This will help you get into the habit of taking your time when fixing problems.

7. Typing in Real Life: Situations You Might Face Think about talking to a friend or writing an email. Kindly type the following sentences: "Hey, how are you? The weekend was great. Let's meet up soon. Would you be interested in getting coffee on Friday?" Touch typing skills can be useful in everyday life if you practice typing in a conversational tone.

Always being the same is important. If you take your time with each practice session, you'll soon be able to type with ease and confidence!

Practice With Paragraphs

Remember to type the paragraph, look it over, and type it again if you messed up. You can't use the delete key.

Zak was a great kid. He looked pretty weak and small, but his strong character made up for it. I had a great time being with him. He was nice and fun to be around.

Jane was really sluggish that day. She was very tired from the great but scary movie she saw the night before. She had a painful headache and her back hurt. It was her choice to ease up.

The event was hard for Jim to remember. He had taken a pretty hard blow to the head and had been out for a while. He wasn't himself for a few weeks afterward, and even then, he got sick and had headaches a lot. He looked pale and waxy.

Practice with Paragraphs

Remember to type the paragraph, look it over, and type it again if you messed up. You can't use the delete key.

We all went to see the pantomime on Christmas Day last year. It was a lot of fun, especially seeing the clowns ride their bikes around the auditorium. When we got home, we were pretty tired, so we watched some black-and-white TV and took it easy.

The shoplifter was caught by Katy and Jacqueline as he was about to leave the store. When they told me about it, they were very excited, and their story made me feel very confused.

In August, I'm taking a vacation to France. I'm getting really excited about it, and I can't wait to take it easy for two weeks while traveling around the peaceful countryside of Provence and Jura. I hope the weather is nice.

Paragraph Practice

CURRICULUM VITAE (CV)

There are plenty of job ads these days that ask for a Curriculum Vitae and an application. The course of your life is what a Curriculum Vitae really means. This word is often shortened to CV, Personal information like your date of birth, address, nationality, interests, etc. should be on your CV. It should also include information about your education, test scores, and any jobs you've had in the past. You should also say if you worked during the holidays. It should also have the names and addresses of two people who can vouch for you, with an employer from the past or present being one of them. Give the names of two people who have known you for a long time and can at least vouch for your character if you have never had a job before. Talk to your Headteacher first. As a matter of course, you should ask the people you choose to be referees first.

First, write a rough draft of your CV. Then, make any necessary changes and then make the final copy. It's worth the trouble to make sure your CV is neat and correct. People who are interested in hiring you will see your CV first, and even if you don't have any experience, a clean, well-organized CV will make a good impression. Of course, you should change your CV as you get more qualifications or work experience.

You should include a short cover letter with your CV that tells the employer where you saw the job opening and why you are interested in it.

THE SECURITY- TASK

Visitors Book

When they arrive, all guests must sign the Visitors Book with their name, address, and the date and time they arrived. When you check out of the hotel, you should write down the date and time you plan to leave.

Responsibility

The hotel is not responsible for things left in rooms that are valuable. There is a safe for guests to use, and there is no fee for this service. For information, please ask at the front desk. It's theft If a guest does, in the unlikely event that they find something missing from their room, they should report it right away to either the front desk or the hotel manager.

Closure of the main entrance

For safety reasons, the hotel's main entrance and front desk will be closed from midnight to 7:00 a.m. every night. During these times, guests who need to get in should ring the bell at the Main Entrance and give the Night Porter their name and room number. Access will be given as long as he is happy.

Awareness in general

When guests leave, they should always be careful with their things and not leave bags and cases lying around in the hallways or at concierge. Also, they should tell Reception or a staff member right away about any strange packages they see. The Manager will question anyone they think is stealing and, if necessary, call the police.

INTERVIEW

During job interviews, which happen quickly, everything is important, even how well you can type. Let's say you got the interview for your dream job and are now sitting in front of a computer for a skills test. What if you could quickly and correctly type out your thoughts? That could change everything.

At this point, touch typing can help you stay quiet. The smooth rhythm of your fingers moving across the keyboard not only shows how good you are at technology, but it also makes you look polished and professional.

Your attention can stay on the content of your responses when you use touch typing instead of fumbling for the right keys. Typing isn't enough; you also need to be able to present yourself professionally and with confidence online. As you get ready for your next interview, don't forget how important it is to improve your touch typing. It could be the thing that makes you stand out in a crowded job market.

Much Longer Piece-Task

While the sun was going down and casting a warm orange glow over the peaceful landscape, Sarah was deep in thought at the edge of the lake. The soft rustling of leaves in the wind and the distant chirping of crickets made a relaxing background for her thoughts. She was amazed by how beautiful nature was and how simple the moment was. She saw a flash of movement and turned around to see a family of ducks floating across the water. Sarah couldn't help but smile as she watched them move in sync.

In that calm place where time seemed to have stopped, Sarah learned how important it is to live in the present. She thought about how everything in life is linked, like how the keys on a keyboard work together to make a whole that sounds good. As she thought about this comparison, her fingers moved smoothly over the keys on her laptop, typing out her thoughts in a way that made them clearer. In the still evening, the steady beat of keys could be heard, a melody of expression and connection.

Touch typing takes time, practice, and a gentle touch, just like appreciating the beauty of the world around us. Learning how to play the keyboard is like exploring the depths of a calm lake. Each keystroke is like a ripple that adds to the whole. So, with a new sense of purpose, Sarah kept typing, enjoying the moment and the way her fingers could move on the keys to express herself.

SUMMARY OF VISIT TO THE LAMPORD HOTEL

When I recently stayed at the Lampord Hotel, I was truly impressed by how well it combined modern luxury with friendly service. The beautifully landscaped gardens and beautiful fountain at the grand entrance set the tone for an unforgettable experience. As soon as I walked into the lobby, I felt at ease because of the beautiful decorations and soothing color scheme.

The people who worked at the Lampord Hotel were incredibly professional and helpful during my stay. Everyone, from the front desk concierge to the housekeeping staff, seemed genuinely interested in making sure that guests not only felt welcome, but also cared for. Checking in was easy, and the front desk staff went above and beyond to tell us about the hotel's features and interesting things to do in the area.

The rooms at the Lampord Hotel are the height of comfort and luxury. They were large, well-equipped, and carefully planned so that they were a peaceful place to relax after a day of exploring. It was clear from the thoughtful touches in the rooms, like the soft bedding and cutting-edge technology, that the hotel puts its guests' comfort and happiness first.

One of the best parts of my trip was eating at the hotel's main restaurant. The food was truly exceptional, with a wide range of dishes featuring flavors from around the world and around the area. Chefs showed that they were experts at what they did by making dishes that were both beautiful to look at and delicious to eat. The atmosphere of the restaurant and the excellent service made every meal a treat.

I was also interested in how committed the Lampord Hotel was to being environmentally friendly. It was clear that the hotel wants to be a good corporate citizen by using eco-friendly methods in its daily operations and starting programs to help the local community. This made me appreciate a business even more because it does more than just provide luxury; it also actively helps the environment and society.

In conclusion, my stay at the Lampord Hotel was wonderful and even better than I had hoped. It's a unique place to visit because it combines luxury, friendliness, and care for the environment so well. The Lampord Hotel is a haven of comfort and sophistication that leaves a lasting impression on its guests, whether they are there for business or pleasure.

CHAPTER SEVEN

OVERVIEW OF MICROSOFT WORD 2021

Introduction to MS Word 2021

Microsoft Word 2021-Get Work Done and Have Fun

When it comes to productivity tools, Microsoft Word stands out as a true classic that is always changing to meet the needs of its users. The 2021 version has a lot of improvements and new features that are meant to make creating documents, working together on them, and formatting them even easier. We'll look at all the important parts of Microsoft Word 2021 in this guide, from the basic features to the more advanced ones, so that users can get the most out of it.

1. Updated the user interface

A new, more up-to-date interface greets users of Microsoft Word 2021. The Ribbon, which is an important part of Word's design, has been slightly changed to make it easier to use. The new colors and icons make the experience look better and be easier to understand. This makes it easier for both new and experienced users to move between the menus and options.

2. Better tools for working together

Microsoft Word has always let people work together in real time, and the 2021 version takes that feature to a whole new level. Users can now work together on documents without any problems, even if they are in the same room or in a different part of the world. When you combine better sharing options with the addition of Microsoft Teams, you can work together more effectively and easily co-author documents at the same time.

3. Writing help powered by AI

In 2021, Microsoft Word will add advanced writing help features powered by AI. The updated Editor tool not only checks for spelling and grammar mistakes, but it also gives you tips on how to improve the style of your writing. Users can look forward to more detailed feedback that will help them improve the way they write and make their documents look better.

4. Smart templates that will help you get more done

One great thing about Word 2021 is that it comes with smart templates. These templates use AI to give you specific suggestions based on the kind of document you're making. These smart templates are great for saving time and making sure that all of your documents look professional. They are flexible enough to fit the needs of any document type.

5. Easy integration of PDFs

Understanding how common PDF files are in today's digital world, Microsoft Word 2021 has improved its ability to work with PDFs. Users can now open and change PDFs right in Word, keeping the layout and formatting. This feature speeds up work because it gets rid of the need for third-party programs to quickly edit PDF files or extract information from them.

6. Improvements to accessibility

Word 2021 puts a lot of effort into making it easier for everyone to use. The new features include better accessibility checker tools and better navigation options. This makes sure that Word documents can be used by a wide range of people, even those who have trouble seeing or thinking.

7. Focus Mode for Writing Without Being Distracted

Word 2021 adds a better Focus Mode because it knows how important it is to be able to focus while writing. In this mode, everything is dimmed except the paragraph you're working on, making it easier to focus after being distracted. Focus Mode helps you get more done, whether you're a student writing an essay or a worker writing a report.

8. More in-depth data analysis with Excel integration

Word 2021 makes it easier for people who work with documents that have a lot of data to connect them to Excel. This lets people add charts and tables from Excel directly to Word documents, keeping the link between the two alive. Any changes made to the linked Excel file are automatically made to the Word document. This makes it easier to present data in a way that is dynamic and connected.

Before opening Word and working on it for the first time you will need to know how to use and control your mouse. Practice resting your hand on the mouse, and use your thumb and two right fingers to move the mouse on your desk. Use your remaining fingers to press the mouse buttons.

There are four main mouse actions:

1 Click by pressing and releasing the left mouse button. This is what you will use most.

2 Double click by quickly pressing and releasing the left mouse button twice.

3 Right click by pressing and releasing the right mouse button.

4 Drag by positioning the mouse pointer over an object on your screen and then pressing and holding down the left mouse button. Still holding down the button, move the mouse to where you want to place the object and then release the button.

HOW TO RUN MS WORD 2021

Setting up and installing

It is very important to make sure that Microsoft Word 2021 is on your computer before you start making documents. The installation process is easy to use whether you have a Windows PC or a Mac.

Getting Around the Interface

Once Word is up and running, it's important to know how to use the interface. We'll go over each part of the workspace, from the Ribbon toolbar to the Backstage View, so you can get used to it.

Making Documents and Formatting Them

You'll learn how to format text, change fonts, and use styles, as well as how to start a new document and import an existing one. Simple formatting tips will teach you how to make your documents look good and professional.

How to Use Pictures and Graphics

In Microsoft Word 2021, images and graphics can be added without any problems.

Working together and sharing

Word 2021 makes it easy for people to work together. Check out co-authoring, commenting, and tracking changes in real time. This makes it easy to work on documents with classmates or coworkers. Find out how to safely share your files on OneDrive or other cloud services.

Getting Good at Themes and Styles

In Word 2021, styles and themes do more than just format text. Learn how to use built-in styles, make your own, and use themes to make sure that all of your documents look the same. Learning different writing styles will make it easier to write anything, from a research paper to a creative project.

Using Macros to Automate Tasks

This goes into the world of macros for people who want to get more done. Learn the basics of recording and running macros to save time and effort when making documents by automating tasks that you do over and over again.

 Tips and Features for Advanced Users

Explore Microsoft Word 2021's more advanced features, like mail merge, making a table of contents, and cross-referencing, to get the most out of it.

How to open MS Word?

The following step shows how to open MS words:

Step 1: Type Ms Word in the search bar.

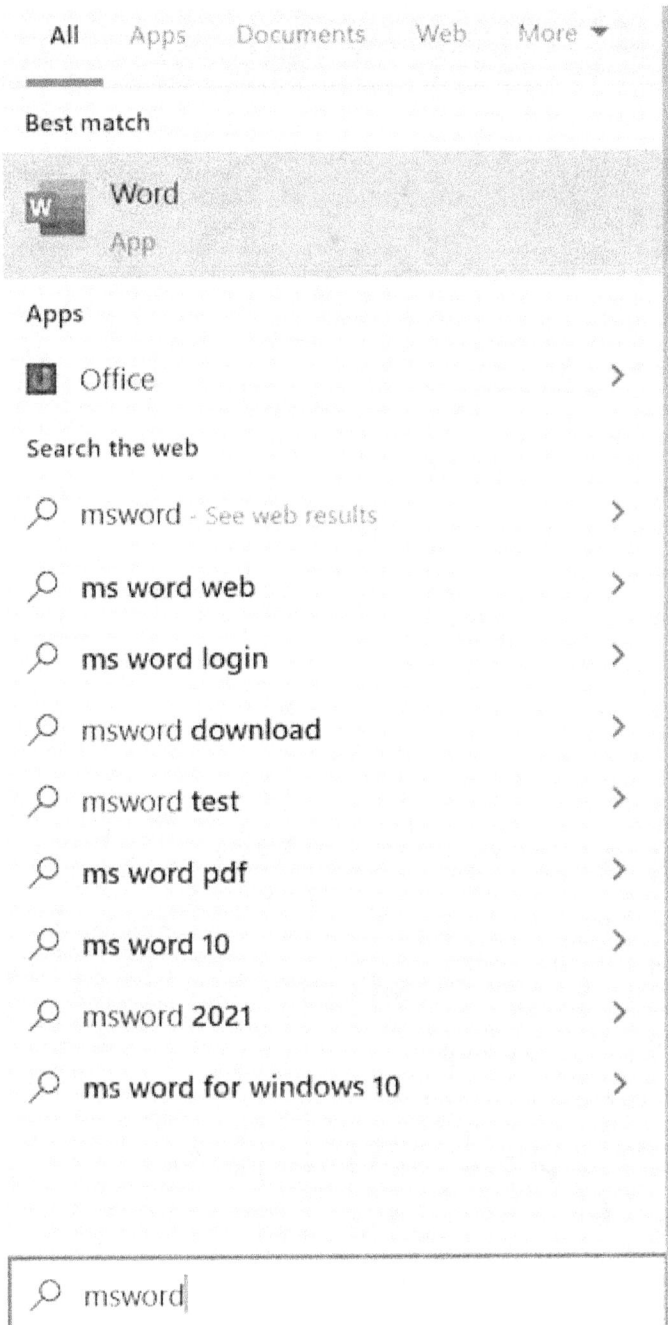

Step 2: Select Ms Word application.
Step 3: Select a blank document and press create button.

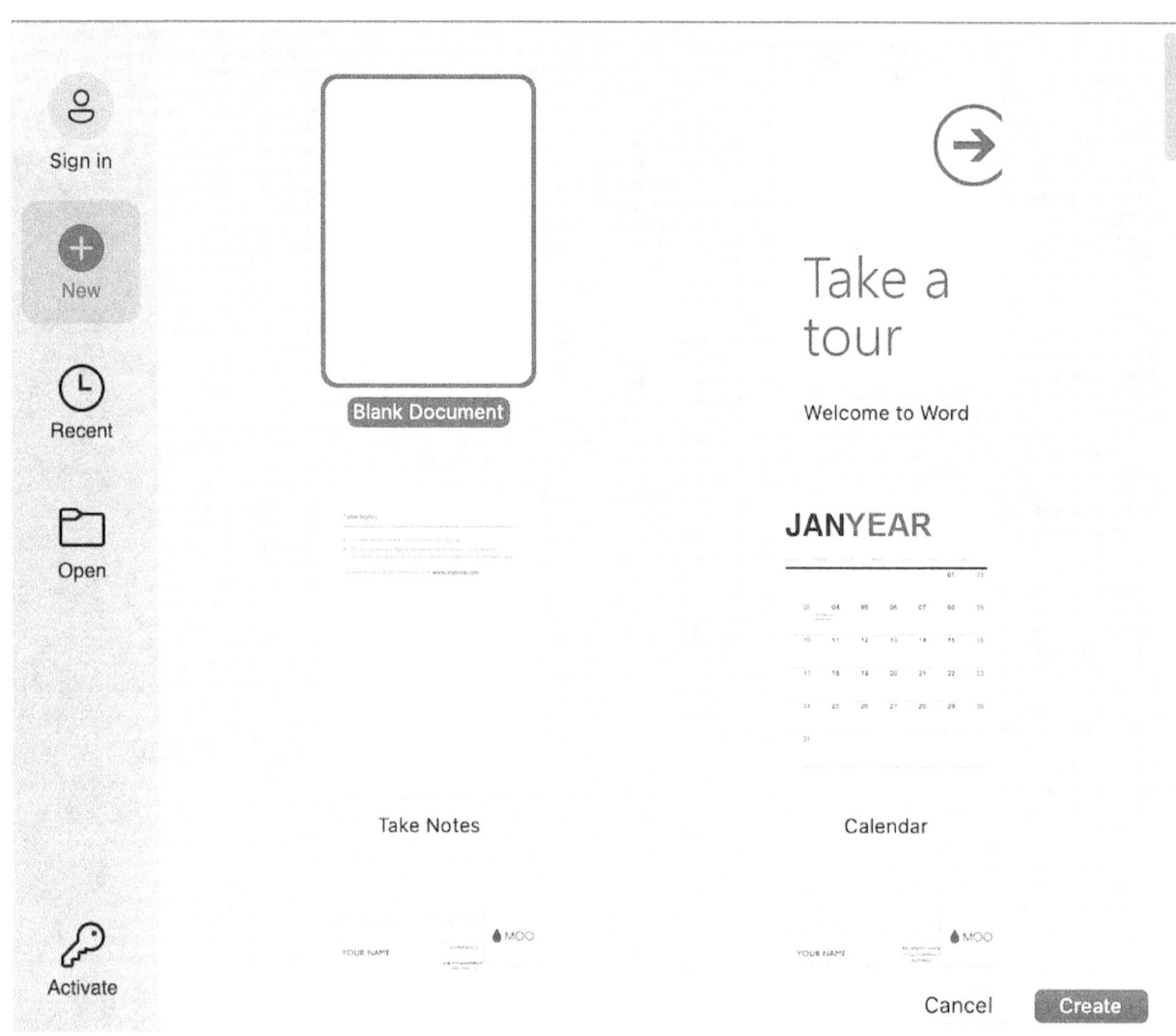

Then you will get a window where you can write your content and perform different types of operations on that content, like font type, style, bold, italic, etc. You can also add images, tables, charts to your document.

FEATURES OF MS WORD

Let's talk about the parts or features of MS Word now. With these features, you can do different things with your documents, such as add to them, delete them, style them, change their content, or just look at them.

1. File

It has options for the file, such as New (to make a new document), Open (to open an existing document), Save (to save a document), Save As (to save a document), Print, Share, Export, Info, History, and more.

2. Home

This is the first tab you see when you open MS Word. It's usually split into five sections: Clipboard, Font, Paragraph, Style, and Editing. It lets you change the text's color, font, emphasis, bullet points, and position. It also has functions like copy, cut, and paste.

When you click on the "Home" tab, you'll see the following options:

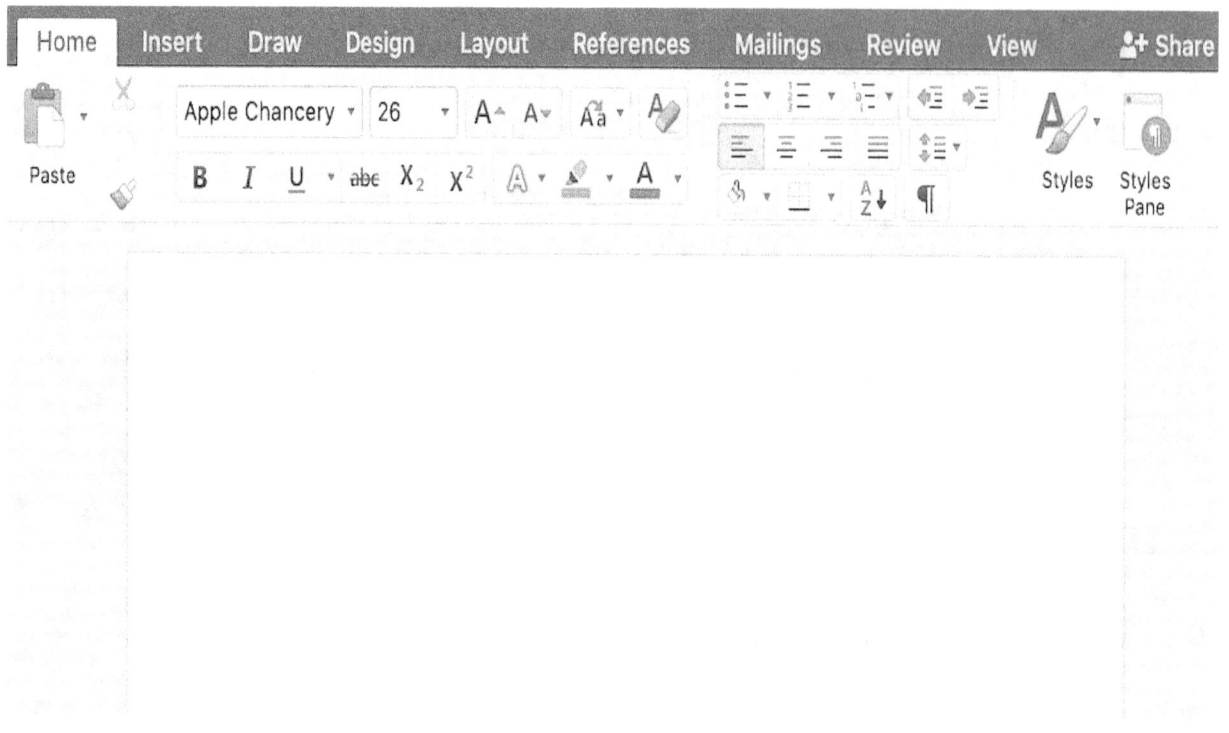

3. Insert

It's the second tab on the ribbon or menu bar. It has different things that you might want to add to Microsoft Word. As you can see in the picture below, it has options like tables, word art, hyperlinks, symbols, charts, signature line, date and time, shapes, header, footer, text boxes, links, boxes, equations, and more.

E.no.	Name	Branch

4. Draw

It is the third tab present in the menu bar or ribbon. It is used for freehand drawing in Ms Word. It provides different types of pens for drawing as shown below:

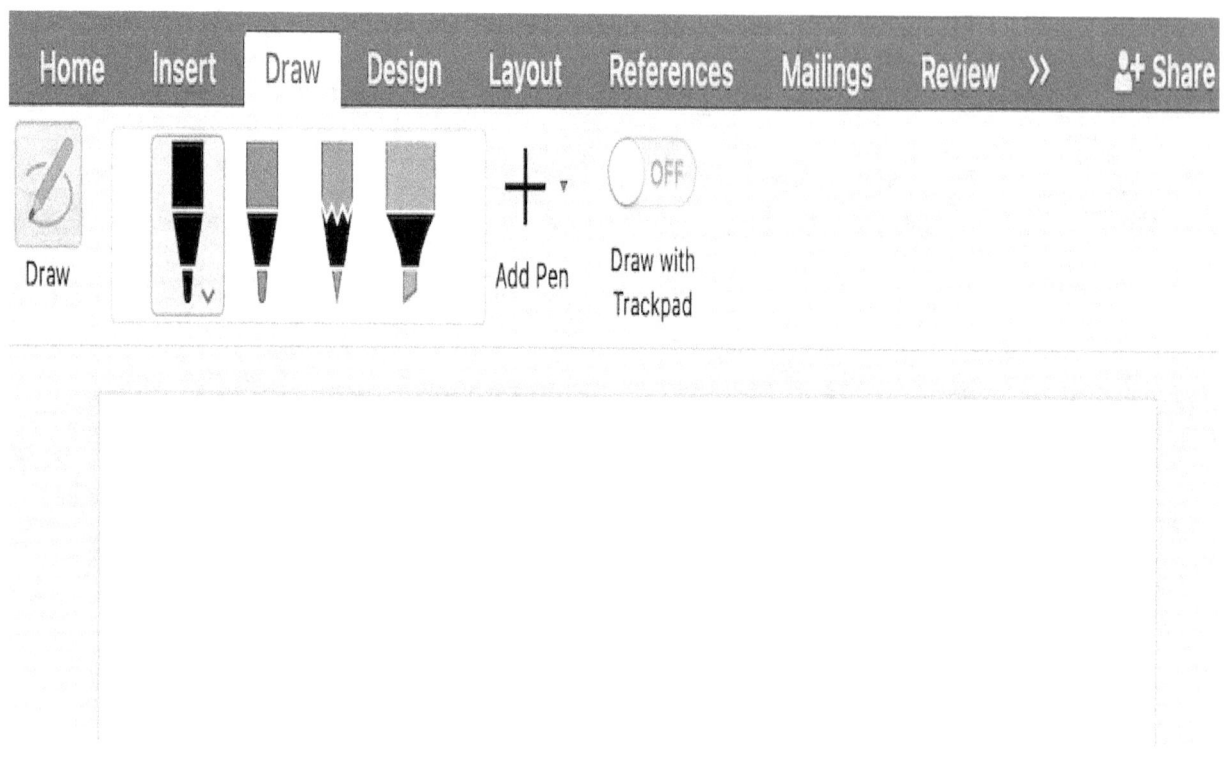

5. Design

It's the fourth tab in the ribbon or menu bar. You can choose from different document designs on the design tab, such as ones with centered titles, offset headings, left-justified text, page borders, watermarks, page color, and more.

6. Layout

It is the fifth tab present on the menu bar or ribbon. It holds all the options that allow you to arrange your Microsoft Word document pages just the way you want them. It includes options like set margins, display line numbers, set paragraph indentation, and lines apply themes, control page orientation and size, line breaks, etc., as shown in the below image:

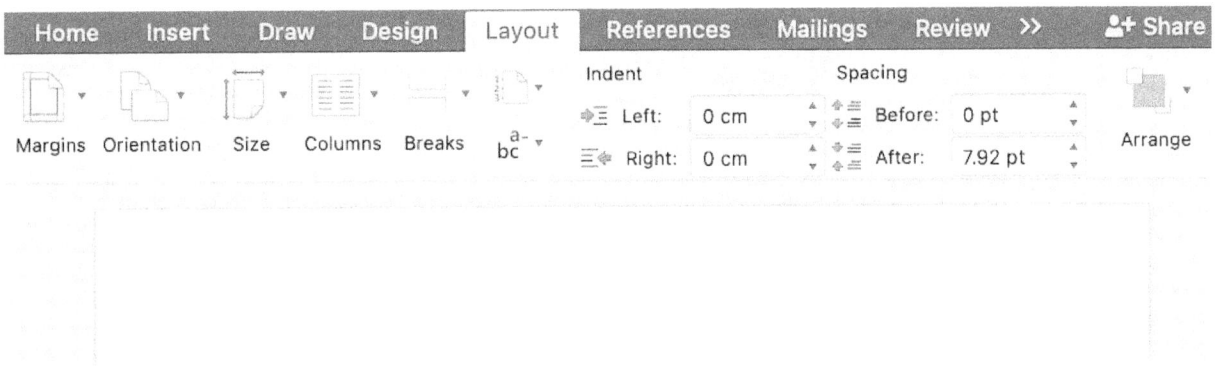

7. References

It's the sixth tab in the ribbon or menu bar. Adding references to a document is easy with the references tab. You can then make a bibliography at the end of the text. The references are usually kept in a master list that can be used to add references to other files. It has features like smart look, index, table of authorities, footnotes, citations and bibliography, captions, and a table of contents.

8. Mailings

It is the seventh tab present in the menu bar or ribbon. It is a least used tab in the menu bar. This tab is where you would create labels, print them on envelopes, do mail merge, etc. After selecting mailing, you will get the below options:

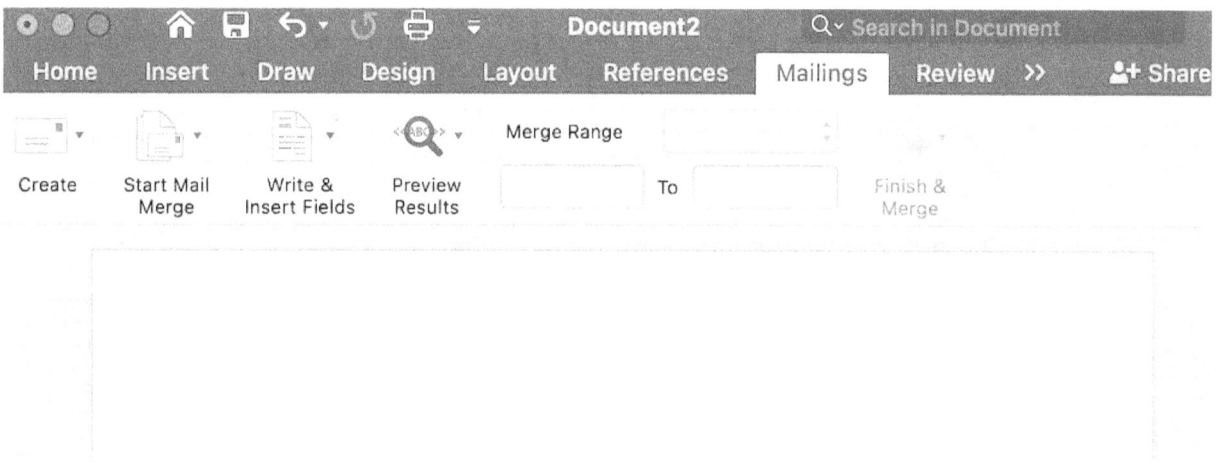

9. Review

It's the eighth tab in the ribbon or menu bar. There are tools for commenting, language, translation, spell check, and word count on the review tab. It helps you find and change comments quickly.

10. View

It's the ninth tab in the ribbon or menu bar. On the View tab, you can choose between single and double pages and change how the layout tools work. The picture below shows some of the things that it has: print layout, outline, web layout, task pane, toolbars, ruler, header and footer, footnotes, full-screen view, zoom, and more.

OPENING SCREEN

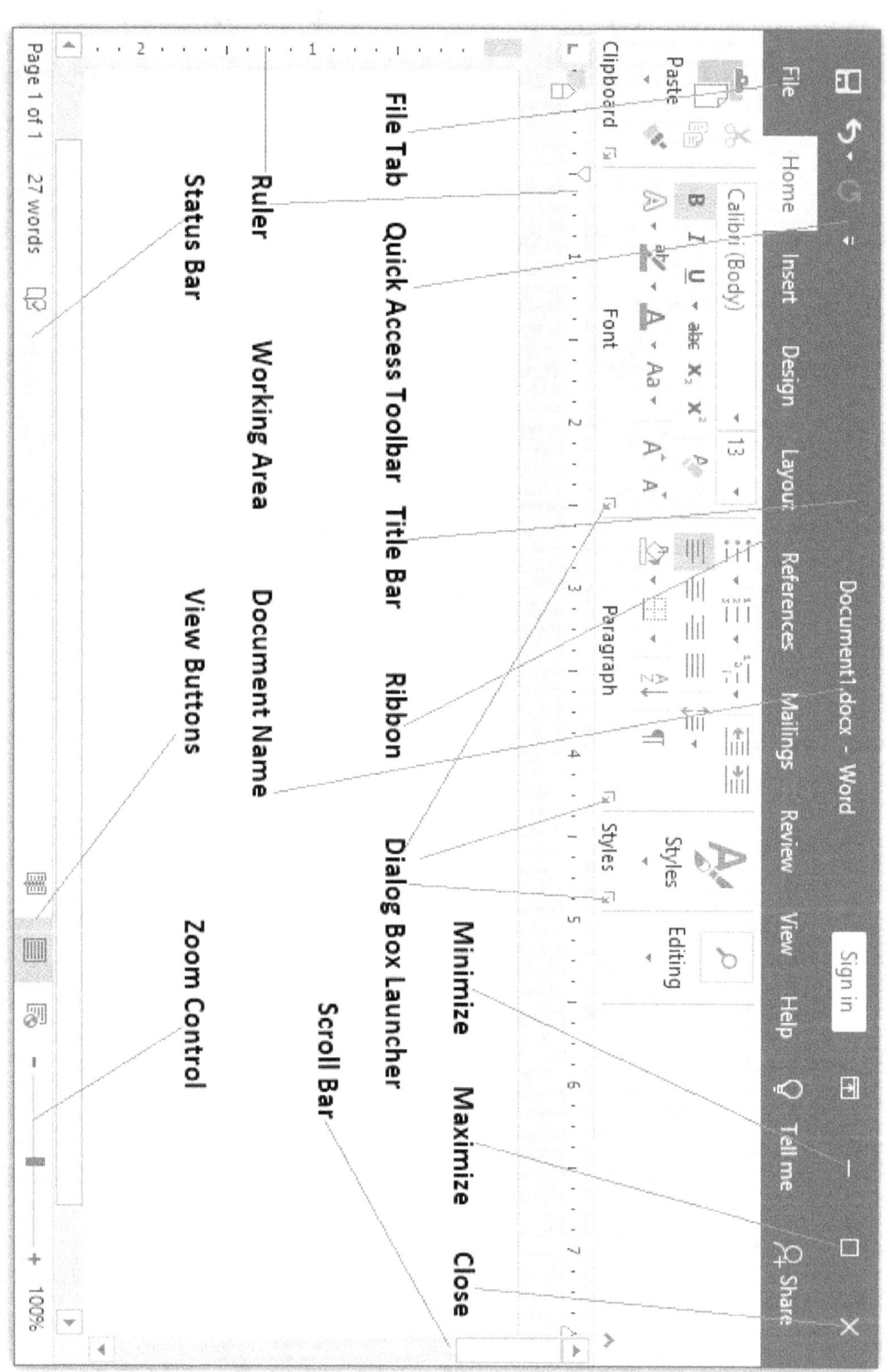

Quick Access Toolbar:

One of the most important parts of the Microsoft Word Window is this bar. It's also at the very top of the screen, in the left corner, right above the File Tab. It's where the commands you use most often go. It's possible to change how this Toolbar looks by clicking the small arrow that shows more options. For example, "New" opens a new document, "Open" shows a saved file, "Undo" undoes the last action, "Redo" does the action again, and "Save" saves the current document.

Title bar: The Microsoft Word window also has a title bar. There is one in the middle and at the top of the document window. It shows the name of the file or program. In that case, we can see the title as Document1 – Word when we open a Microsoft Word file. This is a general name that the program software shows. You can change that name to something more specific to your file when you save it. These are called window controls, and they are on the right side of this bar. You can use it to do three things: minimize, maximize, and close the file or document.

The first one is a "X" that lets us close the Microsoft Word window we are working in. The second part is a double-box icon in the middle of the first two. This icon is used to make the document bigger or bigger. Third, there is a dash "_" icon that we use to make the document we are working on smaller.

File Tab: Out of the Microsoft Office button from Word 2007, the File tab has taken its place in Microsoft Word 2019. On some operating systems, the Microsoft Office button is at the bottom, on the left, and on others, it is at the top, on the left. Click on it to see what's going on behind the scenes. You can see the files you've opened or saved before in this tab. You can also make a new document, print an existing one, and do other things here.

Ribbon of Microsoft Word: The Ribbon is one of the main parts of the Microsoft Word window. It has three layers of organized commands.

Menus or Tabs: These are the horizontal menus that show up at the top of the Ribbon and hold groups of commands that are related. For example, File, Home, Insert, Design, Layout, References, Mailings, Review, View, and Help are all ribbon tabs.
Groups: These are the organized lists of commands that go with each tab or menu. On the Ribbon, the name of each group is shown below the group itself. For instance, a set of commands for a paragraph, the font, or something else.

Commands: As we already said, commands show up in each group. Like, when we press the "File" tab, we see commands or functions like "New," "Open," "Save," "Save as," and so on.

Microsoft Word has two types of rulers: one that goes across the page and one that goes up and down. The ruler on the side looks like it's right under the Ribbon. You can use it to set the document's margins and where the tab stops are. The vertical ruler is on the left side of the document window and is used to find out where things on the page are in relation to each other.

There is a part of the MS Word window called the scrollbar that looks like a long bar and is usually on the right side of the document. It is made up of an open bar with an arrow on it that lets the user scroll faster up and down.

Help icon: You can use the Help Icon to find questions about the Internet. This has helpful guides on how to use different MS Word functions and commands.

Zoom Control Buttons: The zoom slider lets you change the size of the document so that you can view it the way you want. From 0% to 500%, you can widen or narrow the view through it. The zoom controls are a slider that you can move to the left to zoom in or the right to zoom out. You can also click the plus and minus signs to make the zoom factor bigger or smaller.

View Buttons: These are a set of buttons near the bottom of the screen, to the left of the Zoom button. It lets you change between the different views of a Word document.

Print Layout view—This view shows pages just the way they will look when they are printed.

Read Mode: This shows the document in full screen mode.

Web Layout: This shows the document view that you see in a Web browser, like Internet Explorer.

Outline view: This lets you see your document as an outline. We will start by making this view using Word's standard heading styles.

Draft view—This only shows the text of your document, just like it would look on paper. In this view, there are no headers or footers. Open MS Word on your computer to see different parts of the MS

Word window. This is called the document or work area. There is a document or work area where we can type up documents, letters, memos, or just talk to each other. The flashing vertical bar is called the Cursor, and the insertion point shows where you can write text. In general, it's white, and we can see it when we open MS Word. These let the document have more width and comfort.

This is the status bar, which is at the bottom of the document and shows information about the Word file. It shows, among other things, the total number of pages, the number of words, the language, the translator, error messages, sections, and the number of pages.

This bar gives us five different ways to see the document we are working on: print layout, full-screen reading, web layout, and outline view.

Dialog Box Launcher: There is a small arrow in the bottom right corner of many Ribbon groups that show commands. If you click this arrow, a window that goes down will appear with more options about the group.

CHAPTER EIGHT

ESSENTIAL AND WORTHWHILE RULES

Capital letters

When a group of letters or words are in capitals it is best to use the Caps Lock key.

Usually, a light will show that it is switched on. For single capital letters, one of the shift keys should be used.

There are a number of rules for the use of capital letters at the beginning of a word:

◆ Always start a sentence with a capital letter

◆ Always use a capital for the word 'I' when talking about yourself

◆ Use a capital at the start of direct speech

◆ Use initial capitals for names of people, places and proper nouns

◆ Use initial capitals for titles of books, films etc.

◆ Use capitals for days of the week and months of the year, but not for seasons

Look at the following:

The business was called WILLIE BLACK ASSOCIATES.

Four eggs and four teaspoons of milk should be added to the mix.

'The Driver' is the name of Alison Stuart's most recent book.

In July, I'm going to Spain. I enjoy being outside.

Dots and hyphens

For both tasks, the same key is used.

It goes between two words, like in skyscraper, or it goes in place of the word "to," like in 18–20 High Street. There is no empty space on either side of it.

If you need to take a breath or pause, use the dash. A lot of the time, it's used instead of a dot or brackets. There is always room on either side of it.

Take a look at this:

The chairs really did need to have their covers changed.

We plan to be in Kings Street from January 18th to 20th.

I will call you if I have to leave, which is possible.

The show, which was the only one this month, was great.

Exclamation mark

Most of the time, it's used to add humor or stress to a sentence or paragraph.

Take a look at this:

You silly girl! Feel free to trip and fall on the playground.

Well done! You've done so amazingly well.

Question mark

When a sentence asks a question, it ends with a question mark. In business letters, it can also be used to show a question about a date, time, etc.

Take a look at this:

Why are you leaving now? May I join you at the house?

Could you see her? Is she in the front or back row?

At least by February. The letter should get to you by?

Round brackets

When using brackets in a sentence, make sure the sentence still makes sense if the brackets are removed. Generally speaking, the words in the brackets should add some extra explanation to the sentence. Do not use a capital letter for the first word in the bracket, unless for a particular reason. Similarly, a full stop is not needed at the end of the bracketed words.

Look at the following:

Entries (preferably on a postcard) to be sent to us by tomorrow.

Rachel King (the new committee member) will address the meeting.

Important Symbols and General Rules

Square brackets

These are rarely used. Their only real use is to show an addition to a direct quotation:

Look at the following:

Mr. Black said in his report: 'I am so sorry about the lack of pay rise this year, but I hope that you [the employees] will understand the situation.'

Quotation marks

These are used for quotations or direct speech. Either single or double can be used according to preference.

Try the following:

"My project for the year is 'The Rain Storm'," said Tommy.

'I hope you will be able to see our new play "Rafters",' said Marie.

Apostrophes

This is the same symbol as the single quotation mark.

An apostrophe is used for two reasons:

1) To show possession.

The cat's owner lives up the road. (the owner of the cat)

The plural is shown in two ways:

The ladies' shoes were made of leather. (s' apostrophe as 'ladies' ends in s)

The children's shoes were all over the room. (apostrophe + s because the

subject, 'children' does not end in s)

2) To show omission.

An apostrophe can be used to shorten words and is placed at the point where the letters are missing, e.g., don't, won't, I've, it's, you're.

Look at the following:

Sussie's friend was Hyman. Hyman's mum knew Sussie's mum.

Your shoes are the smartest I've seen. They're so cool.

The dog hurt its paw. It's a good thing you were there.

The children's homework is hard. They've got lots to do.

Oblique, solidus or slash

This is used in references or to show options.

Look at the following:

I have the reference to MCD/645 when I typed the letter.

I/we are hoping to show my/our pictures at the gallery.

Ampersand or &

This should only be used in company names, in accepted abbreviations, or in tables where space is at a premium.

Look at the following:

Smith & Jones, together with Brookers & Son, came today.

E & OE, if on forms means Errors and Omissions Excepted.

Numbers

Generally speaking, and unless given specific instructions, numbers can be expressed in either figures or words, so long as consistency is maintained within a document. In newspapers, words are usually used up to 10 and then figures above 10. This is also acceptable.

Sums of money within continuous text

Pounds and pence have a decimal point (full stop) separating them, e.g., £6.50. Always take the pence figure to two decimal places and never type £ and p in one sum. If only pence are involved, they can be expressed as 50p or 50 pence. If only pounds are involved there is no need to take the figures to two decimal places, eg, £12, £14.

Measurements and weights

When typing metric measurements or weights, leave one space after the figures before the unit of measurement. Abbreviations are acceptable. You do not need to add an 's' for a plural.

Examples of metric measurements and weights:

16 mm, 18 cm, 10 kg.

Feet and inches can be written in one of the two following ways:

6' x 4" (using the single and double quotation marks with no space after figures)

or

6 ft x 4 in (leaving one space after the figures)

Note: and 'x' can be used for 'by', eg, 5' x 24".

Temperature

Metric temperature is expressed as degrees Celsius (°C).

Examples of temperatures:

26 °C, 14° – a space is left after the figures if C follows the degree sign, but no space is left

if it does not.

Date

Normally type the date as day, month and year with no punctuation in between:

15 September 2024.

Twelve and twenty-four hour clock

When typing the twelve hour clock, am or pm should be inserted one space after the figures and a full stop should be placed between the hours and the minutes, eg, 9.30 am,

3.00 pm. With the twenty-four hour clock, no full stop or space is inserted in the figures and the times are followed by hrs or hours. There should always be four figures showing

the hours and the minutes, eg, 0930 hrs, 1500 hrs

CHAPTER NINE
TROUBLESHOOTING COMMON MISTAKES

-Identifying and Correcting Errors

-Overcoming Plateaus in Learning

-Practicing with Intent

Correcting Mistakes:

Once mistakes are found, they need to be fixed on purpose. Don't rush through it; instead, look over your mistakes for a moment. Are they caused by speed, accuracy, or a mix of the two? Use typing software or exercises that give you specific drills to help you with the problems you're having. As you practice typing with awareness, you'll slowly start making fewer mistakes and typing more accurately.

How to Get Past Learning Stalls:

There are times when you don't seem to be making any progress when you're learning a new skill. Touch typing is the same. Approaching a plateau with patience and a plan is very important when you find yourself there.

How to Understand Plateaus:

When your brain and muscles need time to get used to learning how to touch type, you may hit a plateau. In fact, it's a normal part of learning and doesn't mean you're not making progress. Knowing that plateaus are only temporary will help you deal with them in a better way.

Tips for Getting Past the Plateau:

If you get stuck, try adding some variety to your practice routine. Try typing at different speeds, with different exercises, or with words that are hard to type. Break up your practice sessions into shorter ones that happen more often. This will help your muscles and mind get used to the new routine more slowly. Remember that progress doesn't always happen in a straight line and enjoy the little wins.

Practicing with a Plan:

Focused repetition is not the way to master something. To really get good at touch typing, you need to practice with purpose and focus. To practice with intent, you need to know what you want to achieve and make sure that your exercises target specific areas for improvement.

Making Goals Clear:

Set clear goals for each practice session before you start. Would you like to get faster, more accurate, or both? Are you focusing on a certain set of keys or words that are giving you trouble? Setting goals gives you direction and makes sure that your practice time is useful.

Targeted exercises are used to:

Instead of typing for no reason, do exercises that will help you reach your goals. If you want to improve your speed, do timed drills. To get accurate results, slow down and focus on being exact. Not only do targeted exercises help your practice go better, they also keep you interested and motivated.

Thoughts on Progress:

Check in on your progress often. Write down what you've accomplished and what you still need to work on. Thinking about your journey helps you improve how you practice and keeps you motivated as you see yourself getting better over time.

Uses of Touch Typing in Real Life Using Touch Typing in Real Life

Communication that works:

• Emails: Respond quickly and write emails quickly to save time and make sure communication is clear.

Use messaging apps to quickly talk to people in real time, whether you're talking about work or personal things.

Making up stories:

• Blogging and Content Creation: Get more done when you're writing creative pieces, blog posts, or articles.

• Writing in a journal: It's easy to write down your thoughts and feelings.

Pursuits in school:

• Taking notes: quickly type up lectures and class notes to help you remember what you've learned.

• Research Papers: Speed up the process of writing school assignments.

Organizing Yourself:

• To-Do Lists: Make and keep up-to-date to-do lists to keep track of your work quickly and easily.

• Writing Down Ideas: Make it easy to remember and organize your ideas for personal projects.

Getting around on websites and software

Work as a professional:

• Data Entry: Excel is good at entering data into databases and spreadsheets with few mistakes.

• CRM Systems: Quickly find your way around and make changes to customer relationship management systems.

Surfing the web:

• Online Research: Type search queries quickly to get more information faster.

• Filling Out Forms: Quickly and correctly fill out online forms.

Coding and Building:

• Programming: Make coding faster and more accurate, which will make development more efficient overall.

• Command-Line Interface: Use this to precisely navigate and run commands.

• Create and share interesting content quickly on different social media sites. This is part of social media management.

• Involvement in the community: Answer comments and messages quickly.

How to Make Work Ergonomics More Effective:

• Good Posture: Keep your back straight to avoid pain when you type for long periods of time.

• Ergonomic Keyboard: Buy a keyboard that makes you feel better and reduces strain.

How fast and how well:

• Regular Practice: Set aside time to practice touch typing every day to keep getting better.

• Use online tools: To improve your typing skills, look into typing games and software.

Keyboard Shortcuts:

• Learn Commands: Get used to using common keyboard shortcuts to quickly move around in software.

• Customize Shortcuts: Make shortcuts work better for you by changing them to fit your needs.

Setting goals for typing speed and accuracy is a good way to keep track of your progress over time.

• Breaks: Take short breaks during long typing sessions to keep your mind clear.

Continuous Learning:

• Stay Up-to-Date: Keep up with changes in technology and touch-typing techniques.

• Online Courses: To improve your skills even more, look into advanced and UpToDate touch-typing courses.

YOUR TYPING SUCCESS

Congratulations on your typing success

When you reach a big goal in touch typing, you should have a party! If you've made a lot of progress, like getting better at the home row or running faster, you should take a moment to recognize it. Celebrating your typing success not only makes you feel better, but it also helps you learn faster.

Taking Note of Progress

Think about the way you've come so far. Take a moment to appreciate how hard you've worked to improve your skills. You might want to keep track of your accomplishments, like when you beat a tough drill or set a personal speed record. No matter how small the step forward is, be proud of it.

Giving yourself a reward

Reward yourself when you reach certain goals. It could be something small like eating your favorite snack, doing something you love on break, or even buying something that helps you type. Reward systems connect good feelings with learning and make the process fun.

Talking About Your Success

Tell your friends, family, or an online community about the things you've done well. When you talk about your progress, you not only feel more accountable, but you can also get helpful advice and support. You could motivate other people to start learning how to touch type too.

Keeping going with your touch-typing journey

The first step is to celebrate your success. As you continue your journey, think about the following ways to keep and improve your touch-typing skills:

1. Practice Over and Over

While it's important to celebrate big wins, the key to long-term progress is consistency. Make time to practice every day, even if it's only for a few minutes. This helps you keep your skills sharp and stops you from going backwards.

2. Do a variety of exercises

To keep things interesting, try out different typing exercises. Type sentences, paragraphs, and even whole articles about different subjects. This not only speeds up your typing, but it also helps you learn new words and ways to put sentences together.

3. Give yourself a challenge

Make new goals to push yourself. Having clear goals for your practice sessions helps you stay focused and on track, whether you're trying to improve your words-per-minute (WPM) speed or work on more difficult typing drills.

4. Look into more advanced methods

Learn more about how to use touch typing. Find out how to use keyboard shortcuts, how to type with your touch, and how to navigate quickly. These advanced skills will not only help you type faster, but they will also help you learn how to use computers in general.

5. Stay up to date

Find out about the newest changes in technology and touch typing. Follow trustworthy blogs, forums, or newsletters that talk about typing and keyboarding. Learning can be more fun if you know about new tools and methods.

6. Join groups for typing

Join online groups or forums to meet other people who type with their fingers. Getting involved with other students gives you a chance to share tips, work through problems, and celebrate group successes.

7. Commit to learning for life

Remember that you can keep getting better at touch typing. Adopt the mindset of always learning, and stay interested in and open to new technologies and techniques that can help you get better at typing.

As you celebrate your progress and move on to the next part of your touch-typing journey, remember that the fun of learning is its own reward. Have fun with the process, keep going, and type away!

CONCLUSION

Your touch-typing journey is complete NOW. Remember to become a skillful and expert typist is all about your newfound comfort and efficiency in digital tasks, not merely speed and accuracy. As you practice touch typing try to incorporate it into your regular life, enjoy the development and don't be disheartened by setbacks. Setbacks are normal, and they enable you to figure out your weakness and helps you grow. Trust your fingers to dance and merry on the keyboard. Your amplified typing skills will help you write emails, documents, and chat with friends. Celebrate and rejoice on your successes, but remember that the trail continues with each keystroke. Happy typing!

Thanks for reading!

www.ingramcontent.com/pod-product-compliance
Lightning Source LLC
Chambersburg PA
CBHW082137290526
45794CB00008B/3066